protect your peace

A 30-Day Devotional for When Everything Feels Loud

The Anchored Devotional Series
Book Three

emery knox

Copyright © 2025 by RMC Publishers

All rights reserved.

No part of this publication may be reproduced in any form, or by any means, electronic or mechanical, including photocopying, recording, or any information browsing, storage, or retrieval system, without prior permission in writing from the publisher.

Under no circumstance will any blame or legal responsibility be held against the publisher, or author, for any damages, reparation, or monetary loss due to the information contained within this book. Either directly or indirectly. You are responsible for your own choices, actions, and results.

Please note the information contained within this document is for educational and entertainment purposes only. All e!ort has been executed to present accurate, up-to-date, and reliable, complete information. No warranties of any kind are declared or implied. Readers acknowledge that the author is not engaging in the rendering of legal, financial, medical, or professional advice. The content within this book has been derived from various sources. Please consult a licensed professional before attempting any techniques outlined in this book.

www.rmcpublishers.com

contents

Introduction	v
Day 1: Not Everything Deserves Your Energy	1
Day 2: Chaos Doesn't Get the Final Word	5
Day 3: Protect the Quiet Inside	9
Day 4: Discomfort Isn't the Same as Danger	13
Day 5: Boundaries Are Brave	17
Day 6: You're Allowed to Log Off	21
Day 7: Don't Let the Noise Name You	25
Day 8: Stillness Is Strength	29
Day 9: Say No Without Guilt	33
Day 10: You're Not a Dumping Ground	37
Day 11: The Holy Pause	41
Day 12: Your Presence Doesn't Have to Be Performance	45
Day 13: You Can Choose Peace on Purpose	49
Day 14: Not Every Fight Is Yours	53
Day 15: Protect What's Holy in You	57
Day 16: Disengaging Doesn't Mean You Don't Care	61
Day 17: Peace Can Be a Protest	65
Day 18: Clarity Is a Form of Kindness	69
Day 19: You Don't Have to Catch Every Ball	73
Day 20: Rest Is Part of Resistance	77
Day 21: Let Go of Proving	81
Day 22: Emotional Sobriety Is Peace	85
Day 23: Come Back to Your Body	89
Day 24: Unfollow for Your Sanity	93
Day 25: You Don't Need to Fix Everything	97
Day 26: Your Peace Is a Priority	101
Day 27: Emotional Boundaries Are Holy Too	105
Day 28: Anchor Yourself, Not Everyone Else	109

Day 29: You Can Exit the Drama 113
Day 30: Peace Is Your Birthright 117

Conclusion: Protect What's Sacred 121
One Last Thing… 123

introduction

Hey you,

Let's take a breath together — the kind that says, *I made it here, and I'm ready for more.*

If you've walked with me through *Hope Anyway*, you've reclaimed your right to believe again. If you journeyed through *Own Your Worth*, you've started to remember who you are underneath the noise. And now?

It's time to protect that truth.

This book is about boundaries. The kind that keep you rooted, not rigid. It's about discernment and knowing what to carry and what to set down. It's about rest, not as a luxury, but as a way of life.

We live in a world that runs loud. It fills your head with opinions and expectations and endless comparisons. And in the middle of all that, it's easy to lose your peace. Easy to forget what's yours to hold and what was never yours to begin with.

Protect Your Peace is an invitation to remember.

To return to steady ground.

To choose stillness over striving, truth over chaos, God's voice over all the rest.

Introduction

For the next thirty days, you'll meet yourself again, not the overextended version, not the one trying to please or perform or hold it all together but the version of you that's quietly strong. Anchored. Clear.

You don't need to have it all figured out. You just need to keep showing up with your questions, your tired heart, your hope that's still flickering even when the world feels too loud.

So take a deep breath.

This space is yours.

Let's begin.

With quiet strength,

— Emery

day 1: not everything deserves your energy

Scripture

"Above all else, guard your heart, for everything you do flows from it." — Proverbs 4:23 (NIV)

Reflection

You don't have to attend every argument you're invited to.

You don't have to carry every cause, fix every misunderstanding, or explain yourself to everyone who demands it.

Your peace is sacred. So is your energy. And not everything deserves access to it.

Proverbs tells us to guard our hearts, not because we're fragile, but because we're valuable. Your heart is the wellspring of your life. What you let into it shapes your thoughts, your actions, your rest, your relationships. So protecting it isn't selfish. It's wise.

There will always be noise: other people's drama, online outrage, impossible expectations. And some of it will be loud enough to make you think you *should* respond, engage, explain, react. But pause. Breathe. Ask yourself: *Is this mine to carry? Is this helpful? Is this holy?*

You don't need to numb out or build a wall. But you can build a filter. You can choose where your attention goes, and what gets to

Protect Your Peace

stay. Every "no" you say to chaos is a "yes" to clarity. Every boundary is a seed of peace.

You're allowed to rest your nervous system. You're allowed to log off. You're allowed to not respond.

You're allowed to guard what God is growing in you.

Journaling Questions

- Where in your life are you leaking energy on things that don't matter?
- What boundaries might help you protect your peace?
- How can you practice discernment instead of defaulting to reaction?

Real Talk Quote

Not everything is worth your energy — some things are just noise.

Breath Prayer

Inhale: I guard my heart

Exhale: I protect my peace

Need a soundtrack for today's reflection?

Scan to listen to *"Peace" by Anna Golden*

Day 1: Not Everything Deserves Your Energy

Creative Anchor

Imagine your peace like a beautifully kept garden. It's not meant to be trampled by every passerby or overtaken by weeds. You wouldn't let anyone walk through it with muddy shoes or plant chaos among the flowers. Instead, you'd create paths, prune what doesn't belong, and post a sign at the gate that reads: *Protected Space.*

That's your inner world. Not everyone gets access. Not every voice gets a microphone. Not every conflict gets a reply. The health of your garden depends on what you allow in and what you kindly but firmly keep out.

Try This

Practice a boundary audit. Write down three places you're overextended. Cross out one, then commit to protecting that space this week.

day 2: chaos doesn't get the final word

Scripture

"You will keep in perfect peace those whose minds are steadfast, because they trust in you." — Isaiah 26:3 (NIV)

Reflection

Chaos is loud. It bangs on the door of your mind at 3 a.m., demanding answers, plans, panic. It tells you the world is spinning too fast, that everything is falling apart, and that you're not enough to hold it all together.

But chaos isn't the truth. It's just the noise.

Peace — real peace — doesn't come from pretending life is calm. It comes from choosing to trust even when it isn't. From anchoring your heart to something deeper than circumstances, steadier than your own strength.

The world may be wild, but you don't have to match its pace. You don't have to spiral just because everything around you is swirling. You can be the still point in a spinning room. Not because you've figured everything out, but because you've placed your trust in the One who already has.

You are not the chaos. You are the beloved. And peace still has the final word.

Protect Your Peace

Journaling Questions
- What area of your life feels the most chaotic right now?
- What would it look like to invite peace into that space?
- How can you practice trusting God even when you don't feel calm?

Real Talk Quote

Chaos may knock, but peace gets to answer.

Breath Prayer

Inhale: I am not my chaos.

Exhale: I rest in His peace.

Need a soundtrack for today's reflection?

Scan to listen to *"Still" by Amanda Cook*

Day 2: Chaos Doesn't Get the Final Word

Creative Anchor

A snow globe in motion — shaken, swirling, unsettled. But if you set it down and let it be, everything starts to settle. That's what trust does. It doesn't erase the mess. It quiets your center.

Try This

Set a two-minute timer today. In silence, place your hand over your heart, take slow breaths, and repeat this: *"Chaos doesn't get the final word. Peace lives here."* Do it again tomorrow. And the day after that.

day 3: protect the quiet inside

Scripture

"Come with me by yourselves to a quiet place and get some rest."
— Mark 6:31 (NIV)

Reflection

Some days, the world is just too loud. Not always in volume, but in pressure — constant updates, nonstop expectations, the buzz of productivity, comparison, and noise. Even when we're not moving, our minds are racing. And peace? It starts to feel like something out of reach.

But Jesus knew the value of quiet. Not just as an escape, but as a rhythm. A necessary part of being human. In Mark 6:31, after a time of intense ministry, He invites His disciples to withdraw with Him. Not to a platform. Not to another task. But to rest. To breathe. To be.

This isn't a call to quit everything or to isolate. It's a reminder that your inner world matters and it needs protection. You don't have to be available to everyone, all the time. You don't have to answer every message, attend every event, or engage every argument. You are allowed to preserve your peace.

Protecting your peace doesn't make you selfish. It makes you wise. When you guard the quiet inside, you can hear God more clearly.

Protect Your Peace

You reconnect with your own soul. You stop reacting from anxiety and start responding from stillness.

So maybe today, peace isn't found in fixing everything or knowing all the answers. Maybe it's found in simply stepping away, even for a moment to let yourself come back home to stillness. That quiet place inside you? It's sacred. Go there. And rest.

Journaling Questions

- What kinds of noise (internal or external) make it hard to feel peace?
- When was the last time you experienced true quiet or rest?
- What boundaries could help you protect the quiet inside of you?

Real Talk Quote

Silence isn't empty, it's where clarity begins.

Breath Prayer

Inhale: I protect my peace

Exhale: I choose quiet with God

Day 3: Protect the Quiet Inside

Need a soundtrack for today's reflection?

Scan to listen to *"Quiet" by Elevation Rhythm*

Creative Anchor

Picture noise-canceling headphones, not because the world goes silent, but because you choose what to tune in to. Protecting your peace doesn't mean escaping life. It means filtering what gets in. Quiet isn't the absence of sound; it's the presence of focus.

Try This

Choose one "noise" to turn down today, whether it's a social feed, an endless group chat, or even your own spiraling thoughts. Replace it with 10 minutes of intentional quiet. See what you notice when the volume drops.

day 4: discomfort isn't the same as danger

Scripture

"Suffering produces perseverance; perseverance, character; and character, hope." — Romans 5:3–4 (NIV)

Reflection

Not every hard thing is harmful. Not every tight space is a threat. Sometimes what feels like pressure is actually growth in disguise.

It's easy to panic when discomfort creeps in. Your heart starts racing, your mind leaps to worst-case scenarios, and everything inside screams: *Get out. Shut down. Retreat.* But God's peace doesn't mean the absence of pressure, it means His presence in the middle of it.

Think about a seed underground. It's buried, pressed in on all sides, totally in the dark. But it's not dying, it's being transformed. Discomfort doesn't mean you're in danger. It might mean you're in process.

The world teaches us to avoid pain at all costs. But faith teaches us to look for purpose in the middle of it. To breathe deep, stay grounded, and trust that you're not being buried, you're being planted.

So the next time everything in you wants to escape the uncomfortable, try staying with it a little longer. Name what you're feeling.

Protect Your Peace

Ask what it's teaching you. Growth isn't always pretty. But it's always worth it.

Journaling Questions

- When was the last time discomfort led to growth for you?
- What's your first instinct when you feel unsettled or stretched?
- How might God be using discomfort to deepen your character right now?

Real Talk Quote

Discomfort is not always a red flag; sometimes it's a green light for growth.

Breath Prayer

Inhale: This tension is temporary.

Exhale: I am safe in You.

Need a soundtrack for today's reflection?

Scan to listen to *"Keep Me in the Moment" by Jeremy Camp*

Day 4: Discomfort Isn't the Same as Danger

Creative Anchor

A butterfly in its chrysalis. Everything looks still from the outside, but inside, a messy, unseen transformation is underway. Discomfort doesn't mean you're stuck, it means something sacred is being formed.

Try This

The next time you feel uncomfortable, overwhelmed, nervous, stretched, pause. Don't rush to numb it or fix it. Instead, write down what the discomfort might be pointing to. What's shifting? What's growing? What's waiting to emerge?

day 5: boundaries are brave

Scripture

"Am I now trying to win the approval of human beings, or of God?" — Galatians 1:10 (NIV)

Reflection

Boundaries are not walls, they're doors with locks, and *you* hold the key.

It can feel scary to set limits, to say no, to step away, to admit you're stretched too thin. You might worry you'll seem rude, selfish, or ungrateful. But boundaries aren't about keeping people out. They're about keeping your peace in.

The truth is, every "yes" you give away costs something. Your time. Your energy. Your mental space. And when you say yes to everything, you risk running on empty, not because you don't care, but because you haven't protected what's sacred.

God didn't ask you to please everyone. He called you to live honestly, wisely, and aligned with Him. That means it's okay to disappoint others if it means honoring what He's placed in your hands.

Setting boundaries takes courage. It might shake up expectations or surprise people used to your "sure, I've got it." But brave people protect what matters. And your peace? Your purpose? They matter.

Protect Your Peace

Journaling Questions

• Where in your life do you feel most stretched or overcommitted right now?

• What would a healthy boundary look like in that area?

• What approval are you chasing and how might that be costing you peace?

Real Talk Quote

Boundaries aren't rejection. They're self-respect.

Breath Prayer

Inhale: I am allowed to pause.

Exhale: I choose peace over pressure.

Need a soundtrack for today's reflection?

Scan to listen to *"Safe" by Victory Worship*

Day 5: Boundaries Are Brave

Creative Anchor

Think of a velvet rope at an event, not to be rude, but to manage flow. It tells you: this space matters. This capacity is full. That's what your boundaries do. They quietly declare, "This is sacred space. Please treat it with care."

Try This

Pick one area of your life where you feel overwhelmed. Today, say one honest no, even a small one. Then write down how it felt and what space it created.

day 6: you're allowed to log off

Scripture

"Make it your ambition to lead a quiet life: You should mind your own business and work with your hands." — 1 Thessalonians 4:11 (NIV)

Reflection

Sometimes the loudest thing isn't the world outside, it's the noise in your feed.

The scrolling. The comparison. The notifications that keep buzzing even when your soul is begging for silence.

You weren't made to be constantly available, constantly aware, constantly performing. God invites you to something deeper. Quieter. Real.

Logging off from social media, the group chat, the non-stop pressure to stay "in the loop" isn't weak. It's wisdom. It's choosing to create space for your own thoughts, your own healing, your own heartbeat.

You don't have to weigh in on every issue. You don't need to perform wholeness online while unraveling offline. The peace you're craving might not be on another post or reel, it might be waiting in the quiet place you've been too distracted to enter.

Protect Your Peace

Today, be bold enough to log off. Be brave enough to protect the sacred, un-optimized parts of your life.

Journaling Questions

- When was the last time you felt truly rested, and what helped you get there?
- What platforms or inputs are draining your peace right now?
- What boundaries could help you engage with tech more intentionally?

Real Talk Quote

Logging off isn't giving up. It's showing up for your life.

Breath Prayer

Inhale: I release the noise.

Exhale: I return to quiet.

Need a soundtrack for today's reflection?

Scan to listen to *"In My Room" by Jacob Collier*

Gentle, introspective. A musical representation of solitude and self-protection.

Day 6: You're Allowed to Log Off

Creative Anchor

Imagine a forest untouched by Wi-Fi — tall trees, soft wind, stillness that doesn't need a filter. That's what logging off can feel like: not disappearing, but returning to where your soul actually lives.

Try This

Log off of one app today for 12 hours. Turn off the notifications, delete it if you have to. Use that time to journal, walk, nap, or simply be. Just you, no audience required.

day 7: don't let the noise name you

Scripture

"He will quiet you with his love, he will rejoice over you with singing." — Zephaniah 3:17 (NIV)

Reflection

There are a lot of voices out there trying to tell you who you are.

Too sensitive. Too intense. Too quiet. Too much. Not enough.

You hear it in algorithms and headlines, in other people's highlight reels, and maybe even in your own thoughts — the ones shaped by past hurt or failure. That noise can be loud. And if you're not careful, it starts to shape your identity.

But here's the truth: You don't belong to the noise. You don't belong to your past. You don't belong to every label someone else slapped on you without knowing your story.

You belong to the One who sees you clearly and still calls you beloved.

You are more than your mistakes. More than your online persona. More than the way you're misunderstood.

God doesn't raise His voice to compete with the world's chaos —

He quiets it. He doesn't demand you hustle to be seen — He sings over you, rejoicing in who you already are.

So today, tune out the noise. Let God's voice be the loudest one in the room. The one that tells you, again and again, that you are known, wanted, and enough.

Journaling Questions

- What labels have you carried that don't align with who God says you are?

- What would change if you let God's voice be louder than your inner critic?

- How can you practice grounding yourself in your real identity today?

Real Talk Quote

You're not who the noise says you are. You're who Love says you are.

Breath Prayer

Inhale: I am known.

Exhale: I am not what they say.

Day 7: Don't Let the Noise Name You

Need a soundtrack for today's reflection?

Scan to listen to *"Name" by Nichole Nordeman*

Creative Anchor

Picture a radio stuck between stations with static crackling, fragments of voices overlapping. Then imagine turning the dial, slowly, until one clear voice breaks through. That's what it feels like when you finally tune in to truth. It's not louder, it's just real.

Try This

Write down three labels or names you've carried that don't serve you anymore. Cross each one out boldly. Then, beneath them, write three truths that God speaks over you instead.

day 8: stillness is strength

Scripture

"The Lord will fight for you; you need only to be still." — Exodus 14:14 (NIV)

Reflection

Stillness is underrated in a world obsessed with speed.

We rush. We scroll. We react. We plan escape routes from our own discomfort as if being still means being weak, passive, or unproductive.

But stillness isn't the absence of strength. It's a quiet kind of defiance. It says, "I don't need to have it all figured out right now." It says, "God is still God, even if I pause."

When the Israelites were stuck at the edge of the Red Sea, fear shouted at them to flee or fight. But God told them to stand still. To trust. To watch what only He could do.

Stillness isn't inaction, it's a bold kind of trust. It's stepping back from the panic spiral and choosing peace. It's unclenching your fists and letting God hold what's too heavy.

Yes, movement has its time. But so does rest. So does waiting without scrambling. Strength doesn't always look like hustle. Sometimes it looks like holy stillness in the middle of chaos.

Protect Your Peace

You don't have to prove anything today. You don't have to fix everything. You are allowed to be still. To breathe. To believe that God is already moving even when you're not.

Journaling Questions

- What makes stillness feel uncomfortable or unsafe to you?
- When in your life have you felt strongest in stillness, not action?
- What would it look like to trust God in the pauses, not just the plans?

Real Talk Quote

Stillness isn't quitting. Sometimes it's the bravest move of all.

Breath Prayer

Inhale: I don't have to chase peace.

Exhale: I can be still and trust.

Need a soundtrack for today's reflection?

Scan to listen to *"Be Still" by The Killers*

Day 8: Stillness Is Strength

Creative Anchor

Picture a mountain lake at dawn. The surface unbothered, reflecting the sky like glass. That stillness doesn't mean nothing is happening below. Life is moving, changing, growing — just quietly. That's you, too.

Try This

Set a timer for 5 minutes. Sit in silence with no phone, no music, no distractions. Just breathe. When your mind wanders, gently return to your breath. Let stillness be your sanctuary, not your enemy.

day 9: say no without guilt

Scripture

"Let your 'Yes' be yes, and your 'No,' no." — Matthew 5:37 (NIV)

Reflection

There's nothing wrong with being kind. But kindness isn't the same as being constantly available, constantly agreeable, or constantly exhausted.

Somewhere along the way, many of us were taught that saying no is selfish. That turning someone down means letting them down. That setting a boundary means you're failing at being "nice."

But saying no isn't selfish, it's honest. It's holy. It's healthy. Especially when your yes would come at the cost of your peace, your rest, or your integrity.

God never asked you to be everything to everyone. And He certainly didn't ask you to betray yourself to keep the peace. Sometimes protecting your peace means disappointing others, and that's okay.

Your no might make space for someone else's yes. Your no might be the reason you don't burn out this week. Your no might simply be the truth and that's enough.

Protect Your Peace

You don't need a long explanation. You don't need to apologize for not stretching yourself thin. "No" is a full sentence, and it's one you're allowed to use.

Journaling Questions

- Where in your life are you saying yes out of guilt or fear?
- What does it feel like in your body when you really want to say no?
- How can you practice saying no with kindness and clarity?

Real Talk Quote

Saying no to something that costs your peace is saying yes to your healing.

Breath Prayer

Inhale: I can say no.

Exhale: And still be good.

Need a soundtrack for today's reflection?

Scan to listen to *"Say It" by Maggie Rogers*

Day 9: Say No Without Guilt

Creative Anchor

Imagine a garden gate. It doesn't swing open for everything that walks by, and that doesn't make it unkind. It makes it intentional. Not everything is meant to enter the space you're growing.

Try This

The next time you feel obligated to say yes, pause. Ask yourself: "If I say yes to this, what am I saying no to in myself?" Then decide. No shame. No guilt. Just clarity.

day 10: you're not a dumping ground

Scripture

"Seldom set foot in your neighbor's house—too much of you, and they will hate you." — *Proverbs 25:17 (NIV)*

Reflection

There's a fine line between being supportive and being someone's emotional landfill. If you've ever felt drained after a "catch-up" that was mostly someone venting for two hours straight, you're not alone.

Let's be clear: you're not cold for setting boundaries. You're not selfish for needing space. Being a kind, loving person doesn't mean being constantly available for everyone's unfiltered thoughts, complaints, or chaos.

Sometimes, people unload their anxiety, anger, or pain onto the nearest person, and if you're empathic and reliable, that's often you. But you were never meant to carry the emotional weight of everyone you know. That's not strength. That's burnout waiting to happen.

Jesus listened, yes but He also withdrew. He went to quiet places. He didn't meet every demand. He wasn't available to everyone at all hours. That's not unkind. That's wise.

Protect Your Peace

You get to guard your peace. You get to choose what voices come close. You get to say, "I'm not the right person for this," or "I love you, but I can't take this on right now." That's not a failure of compassion, it's the practice of self-respect.

Protecting your peace doesn't mean abandoning people. It means refusing to abandon yourself.

Journaling Questions

• Where in your life do you feel emotionally overloaded?

• Who regularly crosses boundaries with their words or needs, and how does that affect you?

• What would it look like to lovingly protect your energy this week?

Real Talk Quote

You can care deeply and still say, "This isn't mine to carry."

Breath Prayer

Inhale: I can hold space

Exhale: Without losing myself

Need a soundtrack for today's reflection?

Scan to listen to *"No" by Meghan Trainor*

Day 10: You're Not a Dumping Ground

Creative Anchor

Picture a door with a do-not-disturb sign. Not closed forever, just saying "not right now." That's you, setting healthy boundaries: still openhearted, but not wide open to everything.

Try This

Practice saying one gentle but firm boundary out loud today, even if it's just to yourself in the mirror. Normalize the sound of your own "no."

day 11: the holy pause

Scripture

"Be still, and know that I am God." — Psalm 46:10 (NIV)

Reflection

In a world that celebrates constant motion — hustle, achievement, instant replies — stillness can feel like failure. But what if it's actually faith?

God doesn't demand our nonstop striving. He invites our presence. He calls us not to prove, but to pause. In this holy pause, we remember who's really in control and it's not us. Stillness doesn't mean passivity; it means active trust. It means creating space to breathe, to notice, to reconnect with what matters most.

The holy pause is where clarity returns. Where the fog starts to lift. Where you can finally hear the whisper beneath the noise: *You're not behind. You're not forgotten. You're held.*

This pause might feel uncomfortable at first, even scary. But give it time. Give God time. Let yourself step away from the pressure to perform and into the peace that doesn't require earning.

You're allowed to stop. And in that stopping, you'll find strength you didn't know you needed.

Protect Your Peace

Journaling Questions

- Where in your life are you rushing without really noticing?
- What fears come up when you try to be still?
- How might God meet you in the pause?

Real Talk Quote

You're allowed to stop. Stillness isn't weakness, it's wisdom.

Breath Prayer

Inhale: I pause in peace

Exhale: I trust God's pace

Need a soundtrack for today's reflection?

Scan to listen to *"Breathe" by Jonny Diaz*

Day 11: The Holy Pause

Creative Anchor

When Maya was little, her grandmother taught her how to shell peas on the porch. They'd sit side by side in silence, the rhythm of their hands keeping time. No phones. No distractions. Just the creak of the rocking chairs and the soft plink of peas dropping into the bowl.

Years later, whenever life spins too fast, Maya closes her eyes and goes back to that porch. That moment didn't fix anything or solve everything. But it taught her this: peace doesn't always arrive with fanfare. Sometimes, it comes in the quiet, when you finally stop running.

Try This

Set a 5-minute timer today. Put your phone away, close your eyes, and breathe slowly. Let the world spin without you for a moment and remember that God holds it all.

day 12: your presence doesn't have to be performance

Scripture

"Go into your room, close the door and pray to your Father, who is unseen." — Matthew 6:6 (NIV)

Reflection

There's a quiet kind of pressure that can sneak into every space. The pressure to show up polished, likable, funny, deep, chill, wise, healed. You're with people, but part of you is performing. You're not lying, exactly, you're just curating. Filtering. Presenting the most digestible version of yourself.

Even in places that should feel safe — church, your group chat, your own mirror — it can be hard to drop the act.

But the truth is, you don't need to be "on" all the time. Not for God. Not for others. Not even for yourself.

Jesus spoke of a different way to show up: no spotlight, no pressure, no audience. Just you and God. Behind a closed door. Off-script. Unfiltered. And in that quiet place, He meets you, not the version of you you think He wants, but the real one.

You don't have to prove anything in that space. You don't have to be interesting, articulate, or inspirational. You just have to be honest.

Protect Your Peace

Your presence isn't a performance. It's a gift. And it's okay if it looks quiet, unsure, or messy. God sees past the filter. And He calls that enough.

Journaling Questions

• Where do you feel pressure to "perform" even when you're just trying to be present?

• What would it feel like to be seen without editing yourself?

• How might a private, honest connection with God shift how you show up in public?

Real Talk Quote

You're not a brand. You're a human being.

Breath Prayer

Inhale: I can show up as I am.

Exhale: I don't need to perform.

Need a soundtrack for today's reflection?

Scan to listen to *"Hide Away" by Ben Rector*

Day 12: Your Presence Doesn't Have to Be Performance

Creative Anchor

Imagine a stage light fading to black and behind it, a warm room with no audience. There's a chair, a soft light, and you. No script. No show. Just presence. Just breathe. That's where the real connection begins.

Try This

Choose one interaction today — with a friend, coworker, or even on social media — where you intentionally *don't* filter yourself. Don't overthink your words, posture, or presence. Just show up honestly and kindly, and without performance. Notice how it feels to be received just as you are.

day 13: you can choose peace on purpose

Scripture

"Let the peace of Christ rule in your hearts." — Colossians 3:15 (NIV)

Reflection

Peace doesn't always arrive quietly on its own. Sometimes, you have to fight for it. Not in the loud, aggressive way, but in the deliberate, everyday choices you make.

You can choose peace when you silence the mental spiral instead of feeding it.

You can choose peace when you walk away from drama instead of joining in.

You can choose peace when you pause before reacting, take a breath, and remember who you are.

Peace isn't passive. It's powerful. It's not denial or avoidance. Its strength, settled deep within you, saying, "I don't have to carry everything." It's letting go of what isn't yours, refusing to live in constant reaction mode, and giving your nervous system a break from being on high alert.

The world will keep trying to convince you that peace is impossible unless everything outside of you is calm. But Jesus taught us to carry peace even in the middle of the storm — to let it *rule* in our hearts, not just visit occasionally.

You don't have to wait for perfect conditions. Peace is not the absence of noise. It's the presence of Christ. And you can choose it. On purpose. Again and again.

Journaling Questions

- What does choosing peace look like in your current season?
- Where do you tend to trade peace for urgency or control?
- How can you make space for peace today, even for just 5 minutes?

Real Talk Quote

Peace isn't passive. It's a daily decision.

Breath Prayer

Inhale: Peace is here.

Exhale: I let it lead.

Need a soundtrack for today's reflection?

Scan to listen to "Let the Ground Rest" by Chris Renzema.

Day 13: You Can Choose Peace on Purpose

Creative Anchor

Imagine a traffic light in the middle of a hectic city. When the light turns red, everything stops. It doesn't ask if people are busy. It just holds its ground. Choosing peace can look like that. Pausing when the world expects you to keep rushing.

Try This

Set a "peace break" alarm on your phone today. Just 3 minutes to pause, breathe deeply, and center yourself. Let it be a reminder that peace isn't accidental. You choose it.

day 14: not every fight is yours

Scripture

"You will not have to fight this battle. Take up your positions; stand firm and see the deliverance the Lord will give you." — 2 Chronicles 20:17 (NIV)

Reflection

You don't have to engage in every conflict that invites you. Not every fight is your assignment.

Not every comment needs a clapback. Not every misunderstanding needs a monologue.

Some battles are better left unfought because peace is more valuable than being right.

In this Scripture, God's people are facing an overwhelming army. And what does He tell them to do?

Stand still. Watch. Trust.

That sounds backward in a world that glorifies hustle, dominance, and constant reaction. But peace isn't cowardice, it's courage. It takes strength to stay grounded when everything in you wants to lash out or defend.

Protect Your Peace

There's wisdom in discernment. Knowing when to speak and when to stay silent, when to show up and when to step back, when to let God fight for you, and let go of your need to control the outcome.

This doesn't mean you never stand up for what's right. It means you don't have to bleed out in every battle to prove your worth or righteousness. Sometimes, the most radical thing you can do is choose calm over chaos.

The fight isn't always yours. But the peace? That's always worth protecting.

Journaling Questions

- What conflict or tension are you currently holding that may not be yours to fix?
- How do you usually respond when you feel misunderstood or attacked?
- What would it look like to let God lead in the middle of your current challenge?

Real Talk Quote

You don't have to set yourself on fire to light up someone else's battle.

Breath Prayer

Inhale: I don't have to fight.

Exhale: I will stand and trust.

Day 14: Not Every Fight Is Yours

Need a soundtrack for today's reflection?

Scan to listen to *"Battles" by The Afters*

Creative Anchor

Picture a warrior laying down their sword, not out of defeat, but out of confidence. Knowing the war is already won changes how you show up. You still stand, but do it from a place of peace, not panic.

Try This

Write down one situation you've been emotionally tangled in that isn't truly yours to fight. Fold the paper in half, place it in a jar or envelope, and say, "This one's Yours, God." Let it go, even if just for today.

day 15: protect what's holy in you

Scripture

"Your body is a temple of the Holy Spirit." — 1 Corinthians 6:19 (NIV)

Reflection

You are not just skin and bones.

You are sacred space.

You carry something holy, not just in a metaphorical, abstract way, but in the real, lived-in reality of your body, your breath, your being.

This world moves fast and asks a lot.

It tells you your body is a machine, a product, a project — something to fix, optimize, or hustle into shape. But Scripture says something else. It calls your body a *temple*, not because it's flawless, but because it's inhabited. Loved. Cherished. Worth protecting.

Protecting your peace isn't just emotional. It's physical, too. It's choosing rest when your body's screaming for it. It's fueling yourself with food that nourishes, not punishes. It's skipping the extra obligation so you can go to bed on time. It's noticing what drains you, and stepping away without guilt.

Protect Your Peace

Because your energy is sacred.

Your capacity is sacred.

Your time, your boundaries, your nervous system are all sacred.

This doesn't mean you never stretch or serve or sacrifice. It means you learn the art of balance. You start asking, "Is this good for the temple?" instead of only, "Do they need me to do this?"

You are not selfish for saying no. You are wise.

You are not being dramatic for needing space. You are discerning.

You are not weak for choosing rest. You are listening to God, who dwells within you.

So today, instead of trying to "push through," try honoring what's holy. Start by honoring yourself.

Journaling Questions

- What parts of yourself have you neglected that might need protection or nurturing today?
- Where in your life are your boundaries being tested?
- What would it look like to treat your body and soul like sacred space?

Real Talk Quote

You don't owe everyone access to your holy ground.

Breath Prayer

Inhale: I am sacred.

Exhale: I will protect what's holy in me.

Day 15: Protect What's Holy in You

Need a soundtrack for today's reflection?

Scan to listen to *"Beautiful People" by Ed Sheeran (Feat. Khalid)*

Creative Anchor

Imagine a candlelit sanctuary. Quiet, reverent, and people speaking in whispers out of respect. Now, imagine treating your inner world like that. Not loud, not rushed, but gently guarded. Let that image guide you on how you move through today.

Try This

Choose one way to honor your body or soul today. Take a long shower, delete a draining app, say no without guilt. Call it what it is: an act of worship.

day 16: disengaging doesn't mean you don't care

Scripture

"A time to be silent and a time to speak." — Ecclesiastes 3:7 (NIV)

Reflection

Sometimes the most caring thing you can do… is walk away.

Not out of apathy, but out of wisdom.

Not because you're cold, but because you've finally learned the difference between being present and being consumed.

You're allowed to choose silence.

You're allowed to stop explaining yourself, stop defending your boundaries, and stop getting tangled in arguments that only drain your spirit.

Silence isn't weakness. It's not defeat. It's discernment.

There's a time to speak truth, absolutely.

But there's also a time to be quiet. To protect your peace instead of proving your point. To love someone without absorbing their chaos. To stay rooted even when the noise around you says, "If you really cared, you'd engage."

But genuine care doesn't always show up loud. Sometimes, it looks like trusting God to do the talking.

Like holding your ground with grace.

Like exiting a conversation to stay emotionally and spiritually safe.

You're not heartless for stepping back. You're just learning that being available for everything is a fast track to burnout. You weren't built to carry every burden or fix every mess. Sometimes love means letting go.

Journaling Questions

- Where in your life do you feel pressure to engage just to prove you care?
- When have you regretted staying in a conversation too long?
- How would it feel to choose silence as a form of strength?

Real Talk Quote

You can care deeply and still protect your energy.

Breath Prayer

Inhale: I am allowed to step back.

Exhale: I don't need to explain.

Day 16: Disengaging Doesn't Mean You Don't Care

Need a soundtrack for today's reflection?

Scan to listen to *"Human" by Christina Perri*

Creative Anchor

Picture a busy train station. Voices, movement, energy. Now imagine stepping into a quiet room nearby, shutting the door, and sitting down in stillness. The chaos is still out there, but you've chosen to enter peace. That's what healthy disengagement feels like, not running away, but stepping into rest on purpose.

Try This

Practice the pause today. When something frustrating or emotionally charged happens, resist the urge to respond immediately. Instead, step outside, take five deep breaths, or journal what you're feeling first. See how silence shifts your perspective.

day 17: peace can be a protest

Scripture

"Do not be overcome by evil, but overcome evil with good." — Romans 12:21 (NIV)

Reflection

There's a lie we often believe, that peace is passive. That it's silence. That it means staying quiet, staying small, staying out of the way.

But peace isn't a retreat. Sometimes, it's a **resistance**.

Choosing gentleness in a harsh world? That's protest.

Loving yourself when culture tells you to shrink? That's protest.

Walking away from chaos instead of fueling it? Protest.

Refusing to match someone's cruelty with more cruelty? Deep, brave protest.

The world will tell you to meet fire with fire, to clap back, escalate, dominate. But Romans 12:21 gives you another way: overcome evil with good. That doesn't mean ignoring harm or pretending everything's fine. It means choosing to respond instead of react. To root your actions in truth, not ego.

Sometimes, peace looks like setting a boundary.

Protect Your Peace

Sometimes, it's choosing rest over rage.

Sometimes, it's refusing to carry what isn't yours.

And sometimes, it's just breathing deeply when everything around you feels like it's shouting.

Peace isn't weakness. It's not denial. It's not avoidance.

Peace is power. And wielding it wisely? That's how you change the world, starting with yourself.

Journaling Questions
- What does "peace as protest" mean in your life right now?
- Where are you being invited to respond with goodness instead of escalation?
- How might peace actually be your strength instead of your silence?

Real Talk Quote

Sometimes the boldest thing you can do is stay soft.

Breath Prayer

Inhale: I will not be overcome.

Exhale: I will answer with peace.

Need a soundtrack for today's reflection?

Scan to listen to *"Brave" by Sara Bareilles*

Day 17: Peace Can Be a Protest

Creative Anchor

Picture an open field after a storm — quiet, still, but not defeated. That stillness? It's not weakness. It's survival. And it's the beginning of new growth.

Try This

Next time someone tries to drag you into chaos, pause. Ask yourself: "Is this mine to carry?" If it's not, choose the peace of walking away.

day 18: clarity is a form of kindness

Scripture

"Instead, we will speak the truth in love, growing in every way more and more like Christ." — Ephesians 4:15 (NLT)

Reflection

Let's clear something up: being clear isn't being cruel.

Too often, we equate kindness with softness, vagueness, or just going along to keep the peace. But peace built on confusion or resentment isn't peace at all. It's delay. And it tends to collapse when things get real.

Ephesians 4:15 flips that script. It reminds us that truth and love aren't opposites, they're teammates. Speaking the truth, with love, is how we grow. How we become more like Jesus. Not by avoiding hard conversations, but by showing up to them with honesty, humility, and grace.

Sometimes clarity looks like saying, "That doesn't work for me."

Or "I care about you, but I need space."

Or even "Here's what I need and here's what I can't give right now."

Protect Your Peace

Clear words don't mean you're unkind, they mean you're respectful. Of yourself, and of the other person. You're trusting them with the truth, not dressing it up to make it more comfortable.

So no, clarity isn't cold.

It's kind.

It's healthy.

It's love, spoken out loud.

Journaling Questions

• When have you held back your truth in the name of "keeping the peace"?

• What would it look like to speak more clearly and lovingly this week?

• Where in your life do you need clarity, either to give it or receive it?

Real Talk Quote

You're allowed to be kind and clear at the same time.

Breath Prayer

Inhale: I speak with love.

Exhale: I stand in truth.

Need a soundtrack for today's reflection?

Scan to listen to *"Honest" by Kodaline*

Day 18: Clarity Is a Form of Kindness

Creative Anchor

Picture this: it's early morning, and you're sitting in your parked car. The windshield is fogged up from the inside. You can barely see what's ahead. You could drive anyway, squinting through the blur, hoping for the best, but it wouldn't be safe. So instead, you reach for a cloth and clear the glass. You pause, wipe gently, and let the clarity settle in.

That's what speaking the truth in love does. It doesn't shatter windows. It just clears them. It removes the blur of assumption, confusion, and unspoken tension. It helps everyone involved see more clearly, drive more safely, and move forward with fewer crashes.

Clarity isn't harsh. It's a kindness you offer both yourself and others, so no one has to guess where they stand anymore.

Try This

Practice one honest, kind response today — no fluff, no backpedaling. Just a true sentence that reflects where you stand.

day 19: you don't have to catch every ball

Scripture

"You are worried and upset about many things, but few things are needed—or indeed only one." — Luke 10:41–42 (NIV)

Reflection

You don't have to catch every ball.

Not every need is yours to meet. Not every message requires an instant reply. Not every task, crisis, or emotional weight belongs in your hands.

But if you've ever been the responsible one, the reliable one, the "go-to" person, this is hard to unlearn. You've been praised for your quick responses, your full plate, and your ability to juggle it all. But even Martha, bustling around trying to do everything for Jesus, was gently reminded that just one thing was needed.

Sometimes, that "one thing" is choosing to be still, to sit down, to let someone else carry it.

You don't prove your worth by overextending. You don't have to be everything for everyone to be loved by God. He's not impressed by your hustle; He's after your heart.

So take inventory. Are you carrying balls that were never yours to catch? Are you juggling things out of fear, guilt, or habit?

Protect Your Peace

You are allowed to let some of them fall.

The world won't break. And neither will you.

Journaling Questions

• What are some "balls" you're currently trying to catch that might not be yours?

• Where are you sacrificing peace in the name of performance?

• What would trusting God with your limits look like today?

Real Talk Quote

You weren't created to catch everything. Let some things fall.

Breath Prayer

Inhale: I don't have to hold it all.

Exhale: God holds me.

Need a soundtrack for today's reflection?

Scan to listen to "Let it All Go" by Rhodes & Birdy

Day 19: You Don't Have to Catch Every Ball

Creative Anchor

Picture a juggler in the spotlight, arms in constant motion. Now imagine the moment they step back, let the balls drop, and walk offstage. The world doesn't collapse. The silence that follows? That's peace stepping in.

Try This

Write down everything you're carrying today—physical, emotional, mental. Then cross out one thing you'll release, even if just for now. Let it fall.

day 20: rest is part of resistance

Scripture

"There remains, then, a Sabbath-rest for the people of God; for anyone who enters God's rest also rests from their works, just as God did from his." — Hebrews 4:9–10 (NIV)

Reflection

Rest isn't just a break in the schedule. It's a boundary. A quiet rebellion against a world that glorifies exhaustion.

We've been taught to equate busyness with worth, to wear burnout like a badge. The culture tells you to grind harder, do more, be "on" always. But God whispers something different: *Rest is holy*. It's not optional. It's not indulgent. It's part of the design.

Sabbath isn't just about a day of the week, it's a mindset. A deep exhale that says, *I am not the source of everything*. It's letting yourself be human again, not a machine.

When you choose rest, you're refusing to let urgency and pressure define you. You're declaring that your peace matters more than constant productivity. You're trusting that even when you step back, the world will keep turning, because it was never all on your shoulders to begin with.

Protect Your Peace

Rest reminds you who you are: loved, not for what you do, but because of Who you are.

Journaling Questions
- Where in your life are you resisting rest, and why?
- What's one small way you can practice Sabbath this week?
- How would it feel to believe that rest makes you *more* whole, not less valuable?

Real Talk Quote

Rest is not weakness. It's a holy act of resistance.

Breath Prayer

Inhale: I release the rush.

Exhale: I welcome rest.

Need a soundtrack for today's reflection?

Scan to listen to *"Rest" by Matthew West*

Day 20: Rest Is Part of Resistance

Creative Anchor

She had always equated rest with laziness.

Growing up, rest was something you earned after the work was done, the house was clean, and the checklist was cleared. So she pushed herself hard. Always producing, always proving. Until one day, her body simply said no. No more pushing. No more hustling for worth. No more ignoring the quiet cry for a pause.

It took burnout for her to finally listen. And even then, rest didn't come easily. At first, she felt guilty when she stopped. Anxiety when she said no. But slowly, painfully, honestly, she learned to honor rest as resistance. Not rebellion against work, but a return to rhythm. A refusal to keep measuring her value by exhaustion.

Now she lights a candle in the evening, not because she finished everything, but because she's finally free from needing to. She's learning that peace isn't the prize, it's the path.

Try This

Set a "Sabbath alarm" for later this week—an hour (or more) to unplug completely. No phone. No multitasking. Just stillness, nature, journaling, or napping. Treat it like an appointment with your peace.

day 21: let go of proving

Scripture

"It is for freedom that Christ has set us free. Stand firm, then, and do not let yourselves be burdened again by a yoke of slavery." — Galatians 5:1 (NIV)

Reflection

There's a difference between *living from freedom* and *chasing approval*. One feels like breath, the other like suffocation.

Sometimes the pressure to prove sneaks in quietly. Maybe it's in the way you over-explain yourself. Or how you say yes when you're running on empty. Maybe it's that voice in your head that says, *You've got to earn your place here.*

But friend, proving was never your calling. You were never meant to be stuck in a performance cycle, hoping someone finally sees your worth. That's not freedom, that's a cage.

Christ didn't free you so you could stay anxious about measuring up. He freed you so you could be rooted. Confident. Whole. So you could live unburdened by the need to convince anyone, even yourself that you're enough.

Letting go of proving isn't about giving up. It's about showing up

Protect Your Peace

differently. Freer. Lighter. Anchored in the truth that you're already loved, already chosen, already enough.

Let that truth do the talking today.

Journaling Questions

- Where in your life are you still trying to "prove" your worth?
- What would it look like to live like you're already free?
- Who or what triggers your need to perform, and how can you step back?

Real Talk Quote

Your worth doesn't need a résumé. It already exists.

Breath Prayer

Inhale: I don't have to prove.

Exhale: I am already free.

Need a soundtrack for today's reflection?

Scan to listen to *"Free" by Rachael Lampa*

Day 21: Let Go of Proving

Creative Anchor

A bird soaring, wings open wide — no map, no destination, just trust in the wind beneath it. That's freedom. You don't need to flap harder to deserve the sky. You just need to remember you're meant to fly.

Try This

The next time you catch yourself over-explaining or over-performing, pause. Take one deep breath. Say aloud: "I release the need to prove. I am free." Let it anchor you back to peace.

day 22: emotional sobriety is peace

Scripture

"Fools give full vent to their rage, but the wise bring calm in the end." — Proverbs 29:11 (NIV)

Reflection

Let's be real: emotions aren't the problem.

It's how we handle them that matters.

You're allowed to feel deeply. To cry, get angry, feel anxious, or overwhelmed. But when our feelings take the wheel and start steering the whole car, that's when peace starts slipping through the cracks.

Emotional sobriety doesn't mean shutting down or pretending everything's fine. It means responding instead of reacting. It means learning how to pause when everything inside you wants to explode. It means taking your feelings seriously, without letting them set the tone for your entire day.

And that's not weakness. That's wisdom.

You can let yourself feel *without* spiraling. You can be honest about your emotions *without* handing them the microphone. It's not about denying what's real. It's about choosing not to be ruled by it.

Protect Your Peace

Peace is powerful. But it's also learned. Practiced. Protected.

And every time you breathe instead of snap, step back instead of rage, or speak truth instead of shame, you're building something unshakable.

That's emotional sobriety.

And that's what peace looks like in motion.

Journaling Questions
- What emotions tend to take over most easily for you?
- How do you typically react and how would you *like* to respond?
- What's one strategy that helps you come back to center when emotions run high?

Real Talk Quote

Not every emotion deserves a front-row seat in your life.

Breath Prayer

Inhale: I can feel.

Exhale: I don't have to react.

Day 22: Emotional Sobriety Is Peace

Need a soundtrack for today's reflection?

Scan to listen to *"Control" by Zie Wees*

Creative Anchor

A thermostat and a thermometer might look the same, but they function differently. A thermometer reflects the temperature around it, rising and falling based on the environment. But a thermostat, on the other hand, sets the temperature. You get to be the thermostat. You don't have to absorb every mood, match every outburst, or escalate with the noise. Emotional sobriety is becoming more like the thermostat: aware of what's happening around you, not ruled by it. You don't absorb the chaos. You choose how you respond. That's peace in practice.

Try This

Next time you feel emotionally stirred — angry, anxious, overwhelmed — pause before responding. Breathe in deeply, and ask: "Am I reacting, or responding?" Choose a response that reflects who you are, not what's happening around you.

day 23: come back to your body

Scripture

"Therefore my heart is glad and my tongue rejoices; my body also will rest secure." — Psalm 16:9 (NIV)

Reflection

When life feels overwhelming, where do you go?

Maybe into your head, spinning through every possible outcome.

Maybe into autopilot, just survive the day, feel later.

Maybe into distraction — scroll, scroll, scroll until the noise drowns out your own voice.

But your body? It never stops speaking.

Tight shoulders. Shallow breath. A racing heart.

These aren't just physical quirks, they're messages.

Your body remembers things your brain tries to outrun.

Part of protecting your peace is learning to come back to yourself fully, to not live only in thoughts or expectations or other people's versions of who you should be.

God created your whole being — mind, spirit, *and* body. You are allowed to rest in it. Be present in it. Reconnect with the sacredness of

Protect Your Peace

your skin, your breath, and your heartbeat. Not because it's perfect, but because it's yours.

You're not just a soul with a body. You're a whole story, told in breath and blood and nerves and quiet knowing.

Come back. You're safe here.

Journaling Questions

- When do you tend to disconnect from your body, and why?
- What does "feeling at home" in your body mean to you?
- How can you show your body kindness this week?

Real Talk Quote

Your body isn't the enemy. It's the house you live in. Treat it like home.

Breath Prayer

Inhale: I am present.

Exhale: I am safe in my body.

Need a soundtrack for today's reflection?

Scan to listen to *"Come Back Home" by Petey Martin ft. Lauren Daigle*

Day 23: Come Back to Your Body

Creative Anchor

Imagine a favorite hoodie — soft, familiar, worn just right. That's what your body longs to feel like: a safe place to return to, not a battleground to escape from. Coming back to your body isn't about appearance, it's about presence. It's about honoring the signals, trusting the cues, and making peace with where you live.

Try This

Pause today and place your hand on your chest. Feel your breath. Say out loud: "This is my body. I choose to be here." Repeat it anytime you feel yourself starting to float away.

day 24: unfollow for your sanity

Scripture

"Whatever is true, whatever is noble, whatever is right, whatever is pure, whatever is lovely, whatever is admirable—if anything is excellent or praiseworthy—think about such things." — Philippians 4:8 (NIV)

Reflection

Your peace is worth more than a perfectly curated feed.

We weren't built to take in hundreds of opinions, life updates, hot takes, and highlight reels every time we open an app. But here we are — tired, triggered, comparing, doom-scrolling like it's a sport.

Social media isn't all bad. It can be beautiful, connective, and even sacred at times. But here's the truth: not everything deserves your attention. Not every voice needs a spot in your head. Not every "follow" means loyalty. You're allowed to protect your mind like it's holy, because it is.

If something online constantly stirs up anxiety, shame, jealousy, or exhaustion, that's your sign. You don't have to keep subscribing to it just to be polite, stay informed, or prove you can handle it.

What you consume shapes your peace. What you see shapes how you feel. What you scroll shapes how you speak to yourself.

Protect Your Peace

Unfollow the chaos. Mute the noise. Block the lies.

And make space for what is true, noble, pure, lovely, and good, even if that means logging off for a while.

Your sanity is sacred. Treat it like it is.

Journaling Questions
- What content online tends to disrupt your peace, and why?
- How do you feel after spending extended time on social media?
- What could you replace screen time with that would nourish your spirit?

Real Talk Quote
You're not rude for protecting your peace. You're responsible.

Breath Prayer
Inhale: I choose what shapes me.

Exhale: I protect my mind.

Need a soundtrack for today's reflection?
Scan to listen to *"I Forgot That You Existed" by Taylor Swift*

Day 24: Unfollow for Your Sanity

Creative Anchor

A messy closet bursting with clothes you no longer wear, things you didn't choose, stuff that doesn't fit anymore. That's your feed when it's not curated with care. Peace begins with a clean-out.

Try This

Take 10 minutes today to go through your social media. Unfollow, mute, or delete anything that doesn't align with peace. You don't owe anyone access to your mind.

day 25: you don't need to fix everything

Scripture

"In quietness and trust is your strength." — Isaiah 30:15 (NIV)

Reflection

Not every problem is yours to solve.

Not every tension needs your mediation.

Not every person needs your rescue.

Some of us have been taught that love looks like constant fixing. That strength means stepping in, smoothing it out, holding it all together, even when we're falling apart ourselves.

But what if strength also looks like *letting go*?

There's courage in recognizing your limits. In trusting that God is still God when you're not managing every moving piece. In believing that people can grow without your constant intervention. In saying, "This isn't mine to carry," and walking away without guilt.

It doesn't mean you're heartless. It means you're human.

Fixing everything is exhausting. Being everything for everyone is unsustainable. But living with open hands — that's freedom.

So breathe. You can show up with love without saving the day.

Protect Your Peace

You can care deeply without carrying it all.

You can trust that God is working, even in the messes you didn't clean up.

Journaling Questions

• Where do you feel responsible for problems that aren't truly yours?

• What would it look like to let go of that pressure?

• How can you support others without overstepping your own peace?

Real Talk Quote

You can love people without losing yourself in the process.

Breath Prayer

Inhale: I am not their Savior.

Exhale: I trust the One who is.

Need a soundtrack for today's reflection?

Scan to listen to *"Fix You" by Coldplay*

Day 25: You Don't Need to Fix Everything

Creative Anchor

A tangled ball of string, not yours, but in your hands. You're trying to unknot something that wasn't yours to hold. Sometimes, the bravest thing is to set it down and walk away.

Try This

Pick one situation you've been trying to "fix" that's draining you. Say (out loud if you can): "This is not mine to carry." Then pray for it and release it. That counts as showing up, too.

day 26: your peace is a priority

Scripture

"Peace I leave with you; my peace I give you." — John 14:27 (NIV)

Reflection

You don't have to earn peace like a prize.

You don't have to wait for everyone to be okay before you breathe.

You don't have to postpone rest until your inbox is cleared and every relationship is mended.

Jesus didn't just wish peace for you — He *gave* it. Freely. Intentionally. As an inheritance.

But too often, we treat peace like an afterthought. We defer it. Dismiss it. Sacrifice it for approval, urgency, or the need to please. And then we wonder why we're exhausted, bitter, or on the edge of burnout.

Your peace is not selfish. It's not a luxury. It's a necessity.

When you start protecting it, you begin to show up differently with more clarity, more compassion, and more resilience. Peace doesn't mean your life is perfect. It means your spirit doesn't get tossed by every wave.

Protect Your Peace

Jesus didn't say, "Peace I'll give when you've done enough." He said, "Peace I give you."

Now. As you are. Right in the middle of it all.

Let it in. Let it stay.

Journaling Questions

• What people or situations tend to cost you your peace the most?

• What boundaries could help protect your peace without cutting off love?

• How would your daily rhythm change if peace came first, not last?

Real Talk Quote

Protecting your peace isn't selfish, it's sacred.

Breath Prayer

Inhale: Peace is my birthright.

Exhale: I choose to protect it.

Need a soundtrack for today's reflection?

Scan to listen to *"Peace" by Bethel Music & We The Kingdom*

Day 26: Your Peace Is a Priority

Creative Anchor

Peace is not a finish line you sprint toward —

it's the steady ground beneath your bare feet when you finally stop running.

It's the cup of tea left warm beside you,

the soft exhale after holding it in too long.

You won't always find it in silence —

but you will always recognize its voice.

Like a tide that returns no matter how far it drifts,

peace has a rhythm.

And the more you choose it —

over urgency, over approval, over performance —

the more it chooses you back.

Let the world rush.

You were made to move differently.

Try This

Make a "Peace List" today. Write down 5 things that genuinely bring you calm, then do one of them before the day ends. Bonus: Say no to one thing that threatens your peace.

day 27: emotional boundaries are holy too

Scripture

"Do not make friends with a hot-tempered person, do not associate with one easily angered, or you may learn their ways and get yourself ensnared." — Proverbs 22:24–25 (NIV)

Reflection

Not every emotion around you needs a response from you.

Not every crisis is yours to carry.

Not every outburst requires your presence, your explanation, or your rescue.

Emotional boundaries aren't cold or cruel. They're compassionate. They help you stay rooted in your own peace instead of constantly absorbing other people's chaos.

Yes, Jesus calls us to love, but not to lose ourselves in the process.

It's okay to notice someone's storm without stepping into it.

It's okay to walk away from a conversation that's gone off the rails.

It's okay to protect your nervous system from people who treat you like their emotional trash can.

Protect Your Peace

You can still love others without letting their volatility rule your inner world.

Scripture isn't vague about this. It says to be cautious about the company you keep, because proximity can influence patterns. When we stay too close to someone else's unchecked anger, it starts to seep in. Before long, we react instead of responding, trigger instead of present, and drained instead of discerning.

Emotional boundaries are holy. They're part of your spiritual hygiene.

You're allowed to walk away from what harms your peace and you don't need a five-paragraph essay to justify it.

Journaling Questions

• Who tends to drain your emotional energy the most, and why?

• What boundary could you set that would honor your peace without dishonoring the person?

• How does God model healthy emotional boundaries in Scripture?

Real Talk Quote

You're not mean for having boundaries. You're wise for knowing where peace ends and chaos begins.

Breath Prayer

Inhale: I can be kind.

Exhale: I don't have to carry it all.

Day 27: Emotional Boundaries Are Holy Too

Need a soundtrack for today's reflection?

Scan to listen to *"Leave Right Now" by Will Young*

Creative Anchor

Picture a swing door at a restaurant kitchen. It only opens when necessary. It doesn't lock everyone out, but it knows how to regulate the flow. Emotional boundaries are like that: flexible, but firm. Protective, not punitive.

Try This

Practice the "pause and protect" rule today: when a conversation starts to feel like too much, give yourself permission to take a breath, excuse yourself, or set a time limit, no guilt required.

day 28: anchor yourself, not everyone else

Scripture

"They will have no fear of bad news; their hearts are steadfast, trusting in the Lord." — Psalm 112:7 (NIV)

Reflection

You are not the lighthouse for everyone lost at sea.

You're not the anchor for every drifting soul.

You're allowed to steady *yourself* without holding the whole ship together.

There's a quiet strength in choosing stability without playing savior. It's not that you don't care. It's that you're learning the difference between empathy and enmeshment, between support and self-erasure.

God never asked you to be everyone's emotional emergency contact.

He never assigned you the role of fixer, rescuer, or permanent shoulder.

What He *did* offer you was something better: a place to stand. A steadfast heart. A peace that doesn't rise and fall with the tides of everyone else's crises.

Protect Your Peace

Anchoring yourself in God means trusting that He holds others, too.

It means believing that you don't have to absorb their panic to prove your love.

It means learning to stay grounded when others are spinning, not out of indifference, but out of wisdom.

So if you feel like you've been holding too much, drop the rope.

Come back to center.

You're not selfish for stabilizing yourself first. You're smart.

Journaling Questions
- When have you confused helping with overextending?
- What makes it hard for you to stay grounded when others are overwhelmed?
- What would it feel like to trust God with the people you care about?

Real Talk Quote
Being the strong one doesn't mean being the sinking one.

Breath Prayer
Inhale: I trust You to hold them.

Exhale: I return to peace.

Day 28: Anchor Yourself, Not Everyone Else

Need a soundtrack for today's reflection?

Scan to listen to *"Anchor" by Skillet*

Creative Anchor

Imagine a stormy harbor, boats swaying wildly, ropes tugging, chaos in the wind. But one anchor holds firm beneath the surface. It doesn't chase the waves. It doesn't leave its post. That's you, when you stop rescuing and start rooting.

Try This

Next time someone brings a problem to you, pause before jumping in. Ask: "Do you need advice, help, or just a safe place to vent?" Let your response come from calm, not compulsion.

day 29: you can exit the drama

Scripture

"Warn a divisive person once... After that, have nothing to do with them." — Titus 3:10 (NIV)

Reflection

You don't have to be the referee in every argument.

You don't have to keep the peace by sacrificing your own.

You don't even have to stay where the tension is thick just to prove you're loyal.

Sometimes the wisest thing you can do is simply leave the room — physically, emotionally, digitally. Not with fanfare or passive-aggressive flouncing, but with quiet clarity: *This is no longer mine to carry.*

The world may have trained you to think that boundaries mean you're cold or unkind. But Scripture doesn't say "tolerate dysfunction endlessly." It tells us to discern when division becomes destruction and to walk away when necessary.

Exiting the drama doesn't make you weak. It doesn't mean you don't care. It means you know your peace is too valuable to keep tossing it into a never-ending fire.

Protect Your Peace

You were not created to manage everyone's emotions, untangle every misunderstanding, or absorb other people's chaos. God doesn't need you to be the fixer, just the faithful one. And sometimes, faithfulness looks like removing yourself so He can do what only He can do.

You are allowed to leave the group chat.

To end the call.

To log off, go quiet, and stop explaining.

That's not avoidance. That's peacekeeping, the sacred kind.

Journaling Questions
- Where in my life do you feel pulled into unnecessary drama?
- What fears come up when you think about stepping back?
- What would it look like to prioritize peace over being liked?

Real Talk Quote

You don't have to attend every argument you're invited to.

Breath Prayer

Inhale: I choose what I carry.

Exhale: I leave what isn't mine.

Day 29: You Can Exit the Drama

Need a soundtrack for today's reflection?

Scan to listen to *"False Confidence" by Noah Kahan*

Creative Anchor

Picture a stage, bright lights, intense dialogue, voices raised. Now picture yourself stepping off it, pulling the curtain closed behind you. The audience fades. The noise quiets. Your breath returns. That's the holy art of stepping away.

Try This

The next time someone tries to pull you into conflict, pause. Ask yourself, "Is this worth my peace?" Practice disengaging with grace — no shade, no speech, just space.

day 30: peace is your birthright

Scripture

"The fruit of that righteousness will be peace; its effect will be quietness and confidence forever." — Isaiah 32:17 (NIV)

Reflection

You didn't have to earn peace, it was always yours.

Not as a luxury. Not as a reward for surviving chaos. But as a birthright, given by the One who calls you beloved.

From the very beginning, God designed your soul for shalom, for wholeness, for stillness, for deep and lasting peace. Not the fleeting kind that comes when everything goes your way, but the kind that roots itself inside you and refuses to be shaken.

This world will try to convince you that peace is conditional: if you work hard enough, achieve enough, please enough people, maybe then you'll feel calm. But God's peace doesn't come from performance, it comes from presence. His.

It's what steadies you when the headlines scream.

It's what anchors you when relationships stretch thin.

It's what whispers truth when your thoughts start spinning.

And the more you protect it, the more it protects you.

Protect Your Peace

So let this be your declaration today:

I was made for peace.

I choose peace.

I carry peace, not just for me, but for the spaces I enter.

You may not control what happens around you, but you get to decide what gets to live inside you. Let it be peace.

Journaling Questions
- What does "peace" mean to you right now in this season of life?
- Where have you been trying to *earn* peace instead of receiving it?
- How can you carry peace forward from here?

Real Talk Quote

Peace isn't a reward. It's a reminder of who you've been all along.

Breath Prayer

Inhale: I was made for peace.

Exhale: I choose to live from it.

Need a soundtrack for today's reflection?

Scan to listen to *"Breathe Again" by Joy Oladokun*

Day 30: Peace Is Your Birthright

Creative Anchor

A river at sunrise — wide, steady, golden with promise. Nothing rushing. Nothing forced. Just flow. That's what your spirit was made for. Not the rapids of panic, not the crashing of noise, but the quiet current of confidence.

Let this be the image you return to whenever the world feels loud: you, grounded in stillness, held by something deeper. Peace was never out there. It's always been inside you, waiting for you to come home.

Try This

Take ten minutes today to sit in stillness — no phone, no music, no fixing, no striving. Just your breath. Just your presence.

Imagine peace not as something you must earn, but something already yours. Let it rise up to meet you. Let it remind you that you've been whole all along.

Then, when you stand up again, carry that peace with you. Not just as a feeling, but as your way of being.

conclusion: protect what's sacred

You made it.

Thirty days of choosing peace — not the performative kind, but the kind that anchors, nourishes, and holds you steady. That's something to celebrate. In a world that demands urgency, availability, and endless opinions, you chose space. Stillness. Clarity. That's holy ground.

This wasn't just about learning to say no. It was about learning what you're saying yes to:

Yes to rest.

Yes to boundaries.

Yes to being whole, not just helpful.

Maybe you started this journey feeling pulled in too many directions. Maybe the noise in your head was louder than the truth in your heart. Maybe you were just tired of pretending to be okay.

But here you are, still breathing, still becoming, still choosing peace. Not just as a feeling, but as a way of life.

That's powerful.

Peace isn't passive. It's deeply courageous. It means knowing what's yours to carry and what isn't. It means leaving the drama,

Conclusion: Protect What's Sacred

the pressure, the shame *at the door* and stepping into your God-given right to exist fully and freely. It means protecting what's sacred — your mind, your spirit, your story.

So what happens next?

You keep showing up differently now. Slower. Softer. Stronger. You create space before reacting. You pause before engaging. You root yourself in what's true and let everything else fall away. You make peace not just a goal but a filter for relationships, choices, and rhythms.

And when the noise rises again (because it will), come back here. Reopen these pages. Breathe. Remember: you don't have to absorb it. You don't have to fix it. You don't have to carry it all.

You are allowed to be soft *and* powerful.

Still *and* strong.

Quiet *and* unshakable.

Peace was always yours. Now it's yours to protect.

So take what you've gathered here and carry it forward into your conversations, your decisions, your rest. Let peace lead. Let it speak louder than fear. Let it remind you of who you've always been beneath the noise.

With all my heart,

— Emery

one last thing...

If this devotional gave you even a moment of peace or clarity,

would you consider leaving a quick review?

It helps more than you know, not just for me,

but for someone else who might be searching for something quiet and steady too.

Just a few honest words can make a real difference.

Thank you for reading.

Thank you for showing up.

With love,

— **Emery**

www.ingramcontent.com/pod-product-compliance
Lightning Source LLC
Chambersburg PA
CBHW060455080526
44584CB00015B/1441